RESILIENCE
THE ABILITY TO REBOUND FROM ADVERSITY

Mark T. Scannell

GASSCANN PUBLISHERS
Minneapolis, Minnesota

ISBN 978-0-9966511-2-7 (softcover)

ISBN 978-0-9966511-3-4 (Kindle)

GASSCANN PUBLISHERS

4556 18th Avenue South

Minneapolis, Minnesota 55407

gasscann@bitstream.net

www.thegratitudeelement.com

DEDICATION

I dedicate this book to four very special people who have had a significant impact upon my life and who have helped me develop greater resilience. The first is Bob Perry, a Dominican priest, a mentor to me in the early years of my priesthood. He is a person of honesty and straightforwardness, as illustrated by an interchange that happened in the early 1970s. Bob and I were in Sioux Falls, South Dakota, leading a parish retreat.

I preached a sermon at the afternoon worship service. While we sat talking that evening, Bob shared with me that he thought my sermon wasn't all that good. I was shocked. Of course, I thought I had done a great job!

He proceeded to say that my sermon was a lot of words with nothing for the people to connect with. He suggested I try using more images and metaphors. I preached again the next afternoon and, though I struggled to feel comfortable trying to use a new approach, Bob affirmed what I had to say.

I learned many things from Bob, and this experience taught me the value of giving and receiving honest feedback and affirmation—two important aspects of developing resilience.

Thank you, Bob!

The second person is Stu Bennerotte, who hired me when I was looking for work after I left the priesthood and was newly married. I was not really sure what I would do, and what I could do. He invited me to work in his company, a manufacturer rep company in the plumbing field.

Stu took a risk to hire me, since I knew very little about plumbing. I learned from him that, at times, becoming resilient includes taking a risk, even when it is unclear whether we will succeed.

Stu taught me important lessons about selling products and about developing resilience. He stressed that selling is never just about the product; rather, it is first and foremost about building relationships with people. He believed that if you remembered details about customers' families and their interests and continually asked about them, the orders would follow. His successes and the successes of his company affirmed his belief. Taking a personal interest in people and building relationships are important ingredients in developing resilience.

Thank you, Stu!

The third person is another Dominican priest and professor, Tom O'Meara. His first Theology class was the first class I took in Theology in 1966. Tom taught me the importance of experience in "doing theology." He brought a new approach to theology as he introduced us to the Protestant theologian, Paul Tillich. (Back in those days, it was kind of revolutionary for Catholics to study Protestant theologians.) Tillich referred to his theology method as correlation. Correlation was bringing together the biblical witness and the work of previous theologians with the contemporary human situation. Rather than just memorize what others have said—a common methodology in those days—and feeding these answers back in exams, the challenge was sizing up the present moment and correlating this with the Bible and the work of other theologians. This opened new doors for me and pointed to the need for ongoing learning, as situations are always changing. Tom helped me to see this added aspect of developing resilience.

Thank you, Tom!

Last but certainly not least, the fourth person is my wife, Elaine. Our lives first crossed in 1970 when Elaine was a Dominican nun, a religious sister; and I was a Dominican priest. Elaine is an artist and certified life coach (as I am). She has taught me a great deal about the vocation and work of an artist. The artist, whatever the medium, is really trying to give expression to their inner thoughts, images, and experiences. For someone like me, who tends to be rather rational, this was a totally different way to experience and express reality. The artist's path presented a challenge that opened a whole new world for me. I could see it was somewhat similar to what Bob Perry challenged me to do with my preaching.

Another key characteristic that Elaine embodies is curiosity, which is an important part of being a life coach. The coach is always curious about what the client is saying, never thinking that s/he "knows." Curiosity is an important aspect of developing resilience, as we shall see.

Elaine and I have been married for thirty-four years, and there have certainly been challenges along the way that have helped us each to become more resilient.

Thank you, Elaine!

CONTENTS

INTRODUCTION

After reading my first book, *The Gratitude Element: A New Look at the Serenity Prayer*, a number of people asked me when the next book was coming. They also asked, "What's it going to be about?" I really didn't have an answer until recently. I have been struck and overwhelmed lately—as I imagine many of us have been—by the very chaotic times in which we are living. There is so much polarization as well as negativity and hatred within and across the various communities to which we belong: the world community, our own country, our churches and families, to name a few. These circumstances are not for the faint of heart!

As we are trying to keep our balance while living in these times, I came upon the energy and dynamism of a particular ability and power called RESILIENCE. I began to hear more about it, read about it, think about it, and talk about it with others. So for those who asked, THIS is that next book! Welcome to the world of resilience!

An important belief of mine, which I explored in some detail in *The Gratitude Element*, is synchronicity.

Simply put, synchronicity is a concept at work in the universe that relates to those apparently random occurrences or experiences that have no obvious causal relationship, and yet they seem to be related meaningfully. We might call them accidents, or we might say they happened by chance. I learned of this "alternative" principle from one of my mentors, Dr. Ira Progoff, who learned of it from one of his mentors, Dr. Carl Jung, who was the first to introduce the concept. Those who embrace this principle acknowledge openness to whatever is happening around us and within us even though it cannot be explained in the usual cause-and-effect way.

Awareness of synchronistic experiences comes from the "brain in our hearts," a term used by Gregg Braden. Synchronicity is that experience that arises from the heart in the presence of meaningful coincidences. Understanding that synchronicity is a "heart" awareness caused me to feel as though I had found something I had been searching for for years. I speak more about this "brain" in our heart and its importance in developing resilience.

This book about resilience was shaped by a number of so-called "accidental" things that happened and that I became aware of as I was writing. For example, one morning in March 2019, I was reading my local Twin

Cities newspaper, the *Star Tribune*, and I found a story with the title, "Minneapolis names resilience chief." Since I was already deep into writing about resilience, the headline caught my eye. What's a "resilience chief"? I immediately wondered, *aren't we all called to be chiefs of our own resilience?*

The article said that the new position was being funded through the Rockefeller Foundation's "100 Resilient Cities" partnership that is "dedicated to helping cities around the world become more resilient to the physical, social, and economic challenges that are a growing part of the twenty-first century." Is your city one of the "100 Resilient Cities"?[1]

This perspective suggests that resilience helps people adapt to changes happening throughout the world, "not just the shocks—earthquakes, fires, floods, etc.—but also the stresses that weaken the fabric of a city on a day-to-day or cyclical basis." Resilience is not only an individual phenomenon but also a phenomenon of the larger societies within which we live. Resilience not only encompasses an individual's way of life, it is also about the way communities come together and live, a hopefully thrive. Resilience is both an individual practice and a social practice.

---

[1] See more at https://www.100resilientcities.org/.

On February 24, 2019, my wife and I were watching the Academy Awards on television when I was struck deeply by the words of musician and actress, Lady Gaga, as she received her Oscar for the song she wrote for *A Star is Born*. Expressing thanks in her acceptance speech, she added, "If you are at home and sitting on the couch, know that this is hard work. I've worked hard for a long time. It's not about winning. What it's about is not giving up. If you have a dream, fight for it. It's not about how often you are rejected . . . It's about how many times you stand up and keep on going." What a great description of resilience!

Lady Gaga's words echoed the sentiments of a favorite wisdom figure of mine, Bréne Brown, whose thoughts are the foundation of a later chapter in this book. In her book, *Daring Greatly: How the Courage to Be Vulnerable Transforms the Way We Live, Love, Parent, and Lead*, Brown talks about leaving the "grandstands" of life and entering fully into life and daring greatly. From this perspective, resilience is about getting up, being willing to fight for our dreams, and not giving up.

At the same time that I have been so focused on resilience, I was deeply affected by the winter weather that was part of Minnesota life this year. We were living in the proverbial deep freeze. We had the snowiest February in

Twin Cities' history, wind chills a couple of days in the range of fifty below, as well as day after day of really cold temperatures that seemed unending. We had heavy snow in April and more light snow in May. There were times that resilience seemed necessary to simply carry out the basic necessities of life.

With the deep chill as a background, two events in February upped my ante for living life more resiliently. The first took place as my wife and I headed out to do our weekly routine of Pilates on a particularly icy day. As I stepped out the back door onto the concrete steps, I slipped, fell, and hit the back of my head. Luckily, my wife was there to help stop the bleeding. We called a neighbor, a nurse, who happened to be home. She came over, looked at the cut, and said I needed to go to Urgent Care.

Once at Urgent Care, five staples were put into my head, and the bleeding was stopped. I was fortunate to have no concussion issues or bleeding in the brain.

The second event took place four days later as I was on an errand to deliver some cookies for a church event. As I accelerated from a stoplight, my car was hit by another car. The side air bags were deployed and, thank-fully, the seat belt did its job. My car made a safe landing on the sidewalk.

Friends who knew I was working on a book on resilience suggested that these experiences were on-the-job training for my topic. I agreed, and I also thought that there would likely be a number of things I'd write about in this book that were part of these accidents. We will always experience accidents in life—some like what happened to me that February, and many more are the stuff of synchronicity. Accidents will continue to challenge us on every level, and our resilience is what enables us to keep moving and getting up when we are down—like on the ice.

I see resilience as a habit, and habits develop through repeated actions. An excellent book on habits and how to change them was written by Charles Duhig, *The Power of Habit: Why We Do What We Do in Life and Business*. One thing that can happen when we try to develop new habits is that we also have to stop doing what we had been doing for possibly a long time. Developing the habit of resilience can mean trying to stop habits like "negative thinking," "giving up" or "playing the role of a victim." Not always so easy!

I see resilience also as a culture—the larger context in which we live. This idea emerged one morning as I was, as usual, reading the *Star Tribune*. A headline read, "Culture of Resilience." The story dealt with a high school in north Minneapolis. Recent shootings near North High School severely threatened the students' feelings of security.

To address students' fears, a team of parents, staff, and community members came together to offer them extra support—in the form of mentoring, help with homework, offering grief counseling, and praying with students. The adults saw these as ways of developing a culture of resilience by seeking to change the culture of fear, hostility, and violence. This is one way to develop a culture of resilience.

By seeing resilience as a culture, resilience is far larger and goes beyond any one individual. It can serve as the backdrop of our lives, which individuals can then build on by their own acts of resilience. This dynamic is really a two-way street: individuals build a culture of resilience, and the culture helps individuals choose resilient ways to live and act. More on resilience as a culture is covered throughout this book.

None of us are spared setbacks, adversities, and even defeats. Resilience is the ability to bounce back and get up after we have been challenged or even knocked out. I offer stories from my experiences with learning resilience as well as those of people who have impacted me, stories that come from my Roman Catholic background and experience, and especially stories about Jesus and his teachings. I find Jesus to be a most resilient person in his humanness. He has much to teach us about developing resilience today.

Each chapter herein describes strategies for developing resilience and begins with the name of a person I consider a "Wisdom Figure"—someone who embodies positive aspects of the chapter's theme.

Each chapter ends with Reflection Questions. A vital aspect of learning is dialogue. I hope you will reflect on the questions and talk about them with others—and tell me what you think too! I invite your feedback by email, text, or in person. My contact information is at the end of the book.

CHAPTER 1

WHAT IS THIS THING CALLED RESILIENCE ANYWAY?

Wisdom Figure: Linda Graham

At the beginning, I feel a need to say something about my own experiences of resilience. I write from the perspective and experience of a white male who has been the recipient of much largesse, generosity, and support from others throughout my life. I want to acknowledge the reality of "white privilege" from which I have benefitted greatly throughout my life. In no way can I match or even come close to the resilience displayed by those members of many minority groups who so often appear to have bounced back from the ongoing discrimination, adversity, setbacks, and obstacles they have been and are confronted with in our culture.

Adversities I have experienced, though real, seem to me to be far fewer than most of my sisters and brothers in racial and cultural minorities. I grieve for their pain and for those who are broken in the struggle, and I also salute the survivors for getting up and bouncing back time after time. I am grateful for the lessons they have taught me. Thank you!

The definition and description of resilience that I want to use fits well with Linda Graham's very practical book about developing resilience. Her book, *Resilience: Powerful Practices for Bouncing Back from Disappointment, Difficulty and Even Disaster,* is filled with many, many practices for developing resilience. Her definition of resilience is the governing definition I use in this book: the capacity *within each of us*—not just a few of us—to bounce back and get up when faced with adversities, challenges, difficulties, and even when faced with defeats.

So, what is it that enables some of us to get up, while others wave the white flag of surrender and don't get up?

I came upon some studies reported in the October 2015 issue of *Science Magazine,* conducted by Dennis Chaney, professor of psychiatry and neuroscience at Mount Sinai Hospital in New York, and Steven Southwick, professor of psychiatry at Yale School of Medicine. In their article in *Science Magazine,* "Implications for the Prevention and Treatment of Depression," they interviewed people who had survived traumatic experiences, such as victims of abuse, prisoners of war, as well as victims of natural disasters. They came to an important conclusion from their research: many people are far more resilient than they think they are, and they have a greater ability to rise to the occasion. What I understand from their research is that expectations are important in relation to feeling resilience. We usually get what we expect! If we believe we can get up from adversity, we stand a greater chance of standing up; if we don't, we probably won't. Keep this in mind as we continue to unpack resilience.

Another important aspect of resilience relates to a Bible verse (Proverbs 29:18), "Where there is no vision, the people get out of hand." We all need a vision and dreams to energize us and keep us going, especially when we are encountering adversities. I am reminded of the speech Dr. Martin Luther King gave in Washington DC, in August 1963—his famous "I have a dream" speech. He mentioned these words eight times in the speech. I believe his dreams and his vision for his people were for all people facing discrimination and adversities. Resilience demands vision, dreams, and a sense of purpose. Without these, we risk perishing.

This connects to the idea of resilience being a habit, which develops through repeated actions; it takes more than just saying we are going to do something differently.

This is why New Year's resolutions are often unsuccessful. We usually choose resolutions (like losing weight, exercising, not drinking) around behaviors that we have been doing for a long time (overeating, doing little exercise, excess drinking). Longstanding habits take time to change, they aren't usually changed overnight. Changing habits and developing new habits take time, and so it is with developing resilience. We need patience with ourselves in seeking to change and develop new habits.

At this point, I will share some of the elements that are part of my vision for developing resilience. The first of these comes from the Bible and concerns the experiences of two biblical characters: Judas and Peter. Both of these men did basically the same thing: they both denied Jesus.

Judas's response: he hung himself. Peter returned and was received back by Jesus. What was the difference? Judas realized what he had done, and he didn't have any hope of being forgiven. He despaired and committed suicide. Peter, on the other hand, returning (I am sure) with some fear and trepidation in his heart, was willing to admit he had made mistakes. He was forgiven. All of us make mistakes and errors in judgment; the question is really, what will we do? Disappear? Or acknowledge what we did and return? Acknowledging mistakes and asking for forgiveness are part of my vision for resilience, which I speak more about in later chapters.

A second element of my vision comes from another biblical passage from Paul's 1st Letter to the Corinthians. This is a reading very often heard at Christian weddings as Paul extols the importance of love and some of the dimensions of love: love is patient, kind, etc. Paul says, "These are three things that last: faith, hope, and love; and the greatest of these is love." (I Corinthians 13:13)

Since I officiate at many weddings and have heard this passage read frequently, I have thought often about what Paul is saying. Permit me to disagree with Paul for a moment. I believe these three—faith, hope, and love—have equal weight. I believe it is impossible to be a loving person without some degree of faith as well as some degree of hope. It is like a table with three legs, and if one of the legs is missing, the table can't stand. Let me explain in more detail how I see faith and hope and love as a vision in developing resilience.

I see faith as encompassing our beliefs, values, and our visions for life and ourselves. Faith is the response to the question: "What do you believe in?" For some, this might entail matters of religion; for others, it might not have anything to with religion and have more to do with spirituality, or work, or politics. Faith often touches on and involves what gives meaning and purpose to a person's life.

Here are some of my beliefs: I believe in the significance of calling a person by name; I believe in the power of like-spirited people coming together to work together and support each other in the pursuit of what is important to them; I believe in the possibility of healing old wounds, hurts, and resentments; I believe in the goodness of people; and I believe that God is a community and we are called to live, work, and create in community; lastly, I believe in the words of the old Frankie Lane song, "I Believe," that promises that for every drop of rain, a flower grows, and somewhere in every dark night, "a candle glows." I see faith and our beliefs as foundational in our lives, giving our lives meaning, direction, and purpose.

The opposite of hope is despair. This despair was significant in my interpretation of Judas hanging himself. He lacked hope of being forgiven and being invited back into circle of the disciples by Jesus. I see hope as really being an indispensable element in developing resilience. Adversities, defeats, and setbacks all challenge our hopes— like having all the air squeezed out of a balloon that is then flat and lifeless. The hopes we have help us hang in there when our beliefs are challenged, when things are difficult, and when there seem to be more questions than answers.

As a lifelong Roman Catholic, I find myself bordering on despair by the sex abuse crisis in the Church and the attempts over many years by the leadership to cover this up and deny what took place. My hopes around this country and the leadership are also challenged by the polarization and divisiveness that is taking place in Washington DC and around the country. What is happening in my Church and in the government of my country challenge my hopes for each. How can I maintain hope without slipping into despair? How can we all maintain hope?

The answer to these questions is crucial in my attempts to maintain resilience—how to stay the course when there seem to be obstacles all over? What gives me hope are people standing up in the face of what is happening and continuing to work for what they believe in—the youth, for example in Parkland, Florida, who have given witness to their fears in protesting the violence caused by the shootings in their schools and pressing for change in seeking to prevent gun violence in schools; the parents and staff at North High School in north Minneapolis, who came together to support their youth in facing the violence that has taken place; people coming together to raise awareness about climate change and to change how plastics are being used and discarded. These grassroots movements challenge what we have tended to take for granted, and they give me hope.

Love and compassion are really the willingness to be affected by the lives of others as well as the willingness to reach out and connect with others. Not to minimize romantic love, I believe that love is a much larger sense of building bridges with others, of connecting with others. It is also a willingness to experience intimacy with others.

I am reminded of the words of Henry Kimsey House, one of the founders of the Coach's Training Institute (now called Co-Active Training Institute) where Elaine and I both studied to become life coaches. House's take on intimacy: "Into me see." Intimacy from this perspective is letting others see into me, and my willingness to see into the inside of another.

I remember the story from the Hebrew Bible where Moses, realizing he was on sacred ground, took off his shoes. When we experience intimacy with others, we are on sacred ground, and it is time to take off our shoes and recognize that we are in a holy place. I delve more into this when we look at how we might deal more creatively with feelings of shame.

So yes, there are three: faith, hope, and love. These three remain and in my view *they are all equally important—* like the parts of a three-legged table.

I want to return to the stories with which I began this chapter—the stories of Judas and Peter. My contention is that Judas, faced with what he did, lost hope and faith in himself and in Jesus, and he hung himself. Peter somehow retained some faith and hope in himself and Jesus, and he returned and was welcomed back; and in the process, he discovered that he had not committed an unforgiveable sin. The only sin that can't be forgiven is giving up hope of being forgiven.

Resilience then is a habit that develops through repeated actions of getting up again and again, even when the odds seem to be against us. This foundation for resilience and the ability to bounce back are ultimately rooted in our vision and dreams for ourselves—like Dr. King having that dream that he spoke about again and again and upon which he acted throughout his life.

Our vision is based upon our values and beliefs, our hopes and our commitment to be loving people. It is clearly important to talk about these fundamental realities in our lives and share these with others.

If we don't reflect upon our beliefs and hopes, they

are at risk of being lost in the ether.

    With that knowledge as a foundation, it is time for me to begin to identify practices that I have found helpful in developing resilience.

    Come along and join me on this ride!

Reflection Questions

Who are your wisdom figures?

Who are some people in your life who have supported you through thick and thin and enabled you to bounce back?

Have you ever tried to change a longtime habit? If so, what helped you? What were some of the challenges you faced?

What are some of your values? What do you believe in?

What gives you hope?

What do you dream about?

What vision do you have for yourself, your life, and the lives of those you love?

How do you love others?

CHAPTER 2

ONGOING LEARNING AND DIALOGUE

Wisdom Figure: George Washington Carver

Synchronistically, as I began writing this chapter, a friend of mine from Church, Glenn Olson, gave me a copy of a book that his grandfather wrote, *The Man Who Talks with the Flowers: The Life Story of George Washington Carver.* Glenn's grandfather was Glenn Clark, who was an intimate friend of Carver. I knew bits and pieces about Carver's life before reading this book, especially his relationship to peanuts. After reading Clark's book, I was further struck by how Carver, as a black man born in 1864, weathered extreme prejudice and innumerable setbacks to receive a college degree and become a college professor. Carver developed multiple uses for the peanut and the sweet potato, and he was a leader in raising concerns about the environment.

The book points out how Carver always had a flower in the buttonhole in his jacket. He would hold a flower in his hand and gaze upon it. He once said, "When I am touching that flower, I am not merely touching that flower. I am touching infinity."

The flower, for Carver, was a doorway that opened into infinity—into a much larger vision of life. This thought correlates with the importance of having a vision for developing and deepening one's resilience.

Glenn Clark speaks about three elements that were part of Carver's vision along with his ability to speak and listen to the flowers and being open to new learning. These elements were: a love of the flowers, his attitude, and lastly, expectancy or wonder. I suggest that these attitudes are very important in terms of what it means to be an ongoing learner as well as someone willing to engage in dialogue with any and every person, animal, and plant.

Everyone and everything can be a teacher if we are open to learning. It was easy to name George Washington Carver as a wisdom figure for this chapter and to see him as an amazing symbol of resilience against large odds as well as being a lifelong learner. Thank you, Glenn, for giving me this book that your grandfather wrote!

Carver's willingness to learn from flowers fits well with the quote by Tao Te Ching, "When the student is ready, the teacher will appear. When the student is truly ready, the teacher disappears."

When we are open to learning, the teacher, whoever and whatever that might be, appears. This also is in sync with the concept of synchronicity—there are no accidents. When we are ready, even though we might not know it, the teacher appears. In other words, don't push aside a possible teacher while looking for someone we think might be the teacher! This is in keeping with the conviction that all of us need to consider ourselves, as well as remain, lifelong learners.

I came to this conviction having experienced many years of formal education and having "succeeded" in that system. The path to my ordination to the priesthood was heavily academic with courses and exams leading to degrees. I have multiple degrees that I was able to acquire by belonging to the religious community that paid for the academic work.

On the one hand, I am grateful for the opportunities that were presented to me; on the other, I want to proclaim that formal education can often stand in the way of true learning. I now see that acquiring a degree is not a signal to stop learning; rather it opens to new possibilities for learning. For a long time, I have been intrigued by the word "disciple"—the term used to describe someone who is a follower of someone who is a master in some field. In

Christian terms, disciples are followers of Jesus. The root of this word disciple, like the root for the word discipline, is the Latin word "disco." Some think this might relate to dancing, like disco dancing. The Latin verb really means "to learn." To be a disciple and to be disciplined means being a learner. In this context, it points to being a lifelong learner. This also fits easily with the view of resilience as a habit. A commitment to learning is a vital part of resilience because there are always so many new things happening as well as so many new challenges to who we are individually and as a people.

An important ingredient in developing the attitude of lifelong learning is another attitude I learned in my life coach training—the attitude of curiosity. I disagree with the old adage that curiosity killed the cat! I rather choose to see curiosity as an attitude that keeps us young and alive. These words of Jesus have always fascinated me: ""Unless you change and become like little children, you will never enter the kingdom of heaven." (Matthew 18:3)

Without curiosity, we risk becoming rigid and frozen. After spending this past winter in Minnesota, I can't imagine anything that would be less fun than ongoing frozenness!

There is a saying often attributed to Albert Einstein

that "doing the same thing over and over and expecting different results is insanity." That's the choice facing us: will it be insanity? Or sanity?

Learning enables us to be flexible in dealing with new and different situations and contributes to developing resilience in facing new challenges. In this vein, I am reminded what Jesus said about judgment, "Don't judge, and you won't be judged." (Matthew 7:1–3) In these words, I hear Jesus saying that there is a different way to look at life and reality other than right vs. wrong or good vs. bad.

I see curiosity as offering a different perspective. Curiosity invites us to see an experience from, for example, the viewpoint of another. Curiosity doesn't mean that everything is the same or that I can't disagree with you. Curiosity is an alternative to the polarization that seems to exist more and more everywhere I turn: I am right and you are wrong. In the halls of Congress, it is a willingness to work across the aisle and not just align with "my people."

Curiosity is a willingness to step outside of myself and walk over, as it were, to see how things look from your point of view. This exercise can help develop some flexibility, which is often necessary in developing resilience.

Think of a tree that is rooted in the soil and at the same time its able to swing and move with the winds that blow through its branches. Resilience is this kind of flexibility that is able to move and adapt to what is happening here and now.

I also see curiosity as a basis for dialogue and for compassion. Both dialogue and compassion invite us to let go of judgments of others, including ourselves, and hear the perspectives of others. For example, as a Catholic, I don't have to give up any of my beliefs in "stretching" to understand the beliefs and viewpoints of Muslims, Buddhists, or any others. I don't know if there is any other way than "stretching" to begin building common ground between people of different persuasions, beliefs, and traditions.

I see two sources for ongoing learning. The first is a willingness to be open to the life experiences of others. It means leaving my "silo" and journeying out to meet people in other silos. There are many ways to do this. I love books. Books (print, ebooks, and audio books) are sources of ongoing learning from others. Also there are online sources such as YouTube videos and Ted Talks. It is important not only to learn more about the traditions in which we have been raised but also those traditions that seem different from ours. The book on George Washington Carver is an example of this and of how much I learned by reading it. I hope this book will be such an experience for you also.

The second source for curiosity and learning is the unique set of experiences each one of us has. What has your life taught you about life? One of my teachers in this regard was Dr. Ira Progoff, who developed the Intensive Journal method of journal-keeping. He developed the method, albeit complex at times, that provided people with an opportunity to value our own life experiences and tap into the unique wisdom that is within each of us. I see a correlation between this method of journaling and developing resilience.

A question can be posed for the journal writer: when were you tested by adversity and how were you able to bounce back and keep going? This is a way for us to tap into our own unique experiences and learn from them.

Every one of us has been tested by adversity, and we are challenged to think of examples of how we were able to be resilient on those occasions. It is important to be reminded and grab hold of these as we continue to experience life and adversities. I am reminded of another saying of Jesus, "Every teacher of the law who becomes a disciple in the kingdom of heaven is like the owner of a house who brings out of his storeroom new treasures as well as old." (Matthew 13:52)

Again there is the link with the disciple, the learner, who is able to bring out of their storeroom their life experiences and memories that can provide insights for what we can do in the present as well as avoid repeating what didn't work in the past. I have seen this happen not only in journaling but also in conversations with trusted people—a friend, a coach, a therapist, spiritual director.

As we share important experiences in the presence of trust and intimacy, all of a sudden "old" experiences speak to us in new ways. I begin to see dimensions I didn't see before. This kind of sharing along with journaling provides ongoing opportunities to learn from our own experiences.

I have seen this happen often with others individually as well as within groups. One group I belong to is a small men's group that I have been part of for probably thirty-five years. John (now deceased), Joel, Gerry, and Dodd meet regularly and share life experiences with each other. There is no judgment. We give each other feedback from our own experiences that often lead to new awarenesses, not only for the individual but for everyone. There is a kind of magic in the air in these group settings.

When the great nondirective counselor, Carl Rogers, began doing counseling, he believed he had his own set of issues and questions. The more counseling he did, the more he began to realize that his issues and questions were those of most people. In some ways, we are not all that unique! What's individual is often most communal. We are more alike than unlike. This is a foundation for us then to be open to learning from others as we share lots of similar experiences. Others have often been there many, many times before us.

The second significant group I'll mention that I have belonged to and benefitted from is a Twelve Step group I have been part of for almost twenty-five years. I have learned with these men that addiction, which can so often be shaming and embarrassing, can be life-giving when shared, claimed, and owned. The crucial components in the atmosphere of this and other Twelve Step groups are the acceptance and support expressed to members, especially when someone shares something very personal.

I have learned that it is difficult to recover from addiction alone. Recovery and resilience are strengthened by the help of supportive people (more about this later).

A hallmark of curiosity is asking questions. In the coaching world, these kinds of questions are called powerful questions. These are questions that are not answered by a simple yes or no; rather they are questions that are open-ended and invite the person to go a little bit deeper into their experience and possibly help the person see something from another perspective. The teacher often shows up as a response to curiosity. My hope is that the reflective questions at the end of each chapter are the open-ended, powerful questions that will enable a deeper look into your own experiences, which you can learn from.

One last thought about ongoing learning and dialogue as a way to develop resilience. The purpose and goal of learning and reflection is wisdom. Wisdom is different from acquiring knowledge or getting credits to earn a degree. Wisdom is more than just collecting information. Wisdom is really the fruit of what our existence has taught us about life—what gives life meaning, purpose, and direction.

This is the kind of wisdom that the Serenity Prayer, the focus of my other book, is interested in acquiring. I share this prayer with the addition of my contribution of Gratitude.

God, grant me the Serenity to accept the things I cannot change;
the Courage to change the things I can;
the Wisdom to know the difference;
and the Gratitude for the Serenity, Courage, and Wisdom you have given me

The learning I am speaking about as an important aspect of developing resilience is really acquiring the wisdom to know the difference, and this can only develop through practice. And don't forget how belonging to a community of people who are committed to learning can be an important part of experiencing a learning culture.

Reflection Questions

As you think about challenging experiences you overcame, what helped you to be resilient?

Where do you learn the best?

Who are your teachers?

How curious are you? What are you curious about these days?

How do you live within a culture of learning?

Who you know who is curious and asks questions that motivate you to learn?

CHAPTER 3

THE IMPACT OF BELONGING
ON RESILIENCE

Wisdom Figure: Gregg Braden

"No *one* is an island." (I altered John Donne's words to be more inclusive.) His words point to the basic reality that we as human beings are social animals. Connected to this is also a basic need, which is TO BELONG. I use capitol letters to signify how important I believe this quality of belonging is. I enjoy playing with words. Here I see "the longing to be" as part of the experience of "belonging." My thinking about this relationship is heightened by the Wisdom Figure of this chapter: Gregg Braden.

In his book, *Resilience From the Heart: The Power to Thrive in Life's Extremes*, Braden explores the relationships between individuals and the communities to which we belong. Through the field of energy within which we all live, we can influence each other and be influenced by others. I owe a debt of gratitude to Gregg Braden for opening my eyes on this topic.

I will share a story that speaks to me about community and which led me to discover Gregg Braden. Around the first of this year (2019), I paid a visit to a "body" therapist (a therapeutic massage therapist) with whom my wife and I have worked for a number of years— Mike Fricke. As Mike was working on me, I simply asked what he was into these days. I asked, knowing that Mike is a curious person and he would probably be into something interesting. Sure enough! My hunch was right.

Mike said he and his wife have been working with a meditation process developed by Gregg Braden. He asked me whether I had ever heard of him, and I said no. He suggested I look at a YouTube video and sample his meditation process. I did that, and I will say more about his process a little later. What really blew me away was that I learned that Braden had written a book on resilience—the very topic I was pursuing. Bingo! More synchronicity!

Can it be that a building block of resilience is a deeper understanding of synchronicity? That is something to consider that I continue to ponder.

In the Yale study of resilience that I mentioned earlier, one of the most significant insights that arose from the interviews with those who had suffered stressful situations was that people are far more resilient than they thought, and they have a greater ability to bounce back than they expected. The study acknowledged a genetic component to resilience; however, the effect was less than expected. Factors we discuss in subsequent chapters, such as exercise, diet, and sleep, are also very important in the development of resilience.

A study led by Heather Rusch of the National Institutes of Health's National Institute of Nursing Research (*Psychology Today*, March 2015), discovered that the two most important factors in developing resilience were having a sense of mastery (the degree to which a person feels control over their life circumstances) and experiencing support. This is consistent with the importance of belonging in developing and building resilience.

Gregg Braden identifies elements he sees as critical for developing resilient communities that can and will support individuals in becoming resilient—the culture in which we live and can find the support we need to bounce back. He speaks about the importance of a common vision, common bonds, and communication. Common visions and bonds evolve when people take time to communicate with each other.

No communication, no community! That has been

my experience in the two groups I described earlier as well as other groups I have belonged to. Basically, we meet regularly to talk and communicate. These bonds can also be developed further by sharing emails and texts. I have found face-to-face meetings to be especially helpful, as well as connecting by phone. Much coaching happens on the phone. And much can be experienced by being attentive to a person's voice.

Back to that study by Heather Rusch: The important dimension of mastery is the ability to see oneself as having some control over our life situation and circumstances regardless of how tragic or difficult they may be. This sense of mastery comes by way of the people we associate with who have positively influenced us, especially family, teachers, coaches, and mentors. We need to be part of communities and groups that teach us how we can feel some control over our life situations and circumstances.

One way we develop resilience is by witnessing other people act resiliently. We often learn through the example of others. Why not teach resilience in schools to young people as a life skill? Resilience is truly a life skill that can easily be taught, especially to young people, as they acquire skills to live productive and creative lives.

An awareness I had around this sense of belonging

was a result of asking where people feel a sense of belonging these days. Articles abound that church attendance is down, whatever the denomination, and this includes Roman Catholic Churches. Often in my role as a wedding officiant, I am invited to carry out this official duty at weddings wherein one member of the couple has a connection of some sort to the Catholic Church. So they want some kind of Catholic presence, often to please a mother or grandmother; and I am the guy because I used to be a priest. The couple themselves had no real desire to connect with a Roman Catholic Church.

The times they are a' changing!

So my question is really more about where people these days are finding communities of *any* kind that support them in their pursuit of what is important to them. Where can people find groups that support them in their wanting to bounce back from adversities and challenges?

Certainly there are support groups for all kinds of issues as well as an assortment of Twelve Step groups. But where else can people find groups that provide a culture that can help them behave or learn to behave resiliently? Where can people go to learn these vital skills?

I had a rather eccentric professor in the mid-1960s, John Dominic Corcoran. His focus was on the field of psychology (and there were also questions raised regularly about his sanity!) and his teaching style was to read passages from the latest books on the topic and toss out his own gems of wisdom along the way.

One day his gem dealt with the meaning of community, and I have held onto this wisdom for some fifty-five years. He said in passing that community had two roots: the first root is communion (from the Latin word *communio*) and the unity between the people who are part of this community. The second root comes from the Latin root *munus*, meaning "task." There are two meanings from these different roots: the importance and focus of unity between the group members (sounds like Gregg Braden), and that this unity grows out of and is expressed within common tasks and works.

Communities don't exist without a purpose. Belonging is about finding ways to experience a unity of purpose by having tasks to do as well as having a mission of some sort.

Jesus said, "Where two or three meet in my name, I shall be there with them." (Matthew 18:20) Two or three are the smallest number that we can have and still be a group. I like this passage especially because it reinforces that communities do not have to be huge in number. They can be small and still be very powerful. My very valuable men's group has been four in number.

So don't worry about numbers. Find like-spirited people who will support you and strengthen you in your desires to be resilient. It just takes one other!

Reflection Questions

Do you belong to a community or communities that help you be resilient?

Do the communities you belong to spend time communicating and developing common visions and bonds?

Did anyone teach you life skills that include resiliency?

Can you teach others about what it takes to be resilient? Are you willing?

CHAPTER 4

SELF-CARE AND SELF-PRACTICE

Wisdom Figures: Michelle Obama and Bréne Brown

When I was first diving into the topic of self-care and practice as important components of resilience, a friend mentioned that I should read Michelle Obama's memoir, *Becoming*. I did, and it was a very good read.

In many ways, Michelle embodies the exchange between Jesus and a Pharisee who asked Jesus, "Master, which is the greatest commandment of the Law?" Jesus said, "You must love the Lord your God with all your heart, with all your soul and with all your mind. This is the greatest and the first commandment. The second resembles it: You must love your neighbor as yourself." (Matthew 22:34–39)

This is the challenge of loving not only God but our neighbors and ourselves. This is another example of the three-legged table: God, neighbors, and ourselves. If one of the legs is missing, the table cannot stand. Michelle continually struggled to balance her life as a professional woman, a wife, a mother of two daughters, a sister, a First Lady, and taking care of herself. Certainly, a full plate!

The struggle grew even greater after Barack was elected president. She battled continually with the expectations she felt were associated with every one of the roles she played in her life. I think Michelle is truly an example, as is her husband, of trying to balance so many aspects of life and still keep in focus the need for self-care and self-practice in seeking to be resilient people.

Jesus's words about love include the reference to self-love, which includes both self-care and self-practice. I include self-practice because self-care is not something we can do only once in a while if we want to become proficient at it. This idea returns to the nature of habit, which comes about through practice—regular practice.

I stumbled upon an article, *Neuroplasticity,* by Mike Rinder on his blog. Mike is a certified neurosculpting facilitator at the Neurosculpting Institute in Denver, Colorado. He speaks about what happens in our brain when we regularly practice a certain behavior.

Our brain is composed of neural pathways, and these pathways become dedicated to a thought or pattern of thinking. If we stop thinking a particular thought, or pattern of thinking, it will become less accessible. When we regularly practice a pattern or a thought, the neural pathway becomes more accessible, and our practice becomes more efficient.

In seeking to change habits, we are seeking to develop new, healthier neural pathways. Mike concludes this article with a couple of important rules of thumb: first, with our neural pathways, it's "Use it or lose it." The most important key to success is: *Repetition! Repetition! Repetition!* Second, we do not automatically change, nor can we expect change, simply because we have knowledge. "The principles of usage require a practice with repetition."

There is no substitute for regular practice in developing habits of self-care, self-practice, and resiliency. This regular practice has an enormous impact upon our brains and touches upon the intimate relationship between our body and our brain. They are not two separate worlds. Only when they work together can they enable us to develop healthy practices of living and loving.

We become what we practice!

I will focus on the importance of loving and affirming ourselves. We do not want to forget the other two legs of Jesus's teaching on love. Self-love and self-care without love for others leads to arrogance, feelings of entitlement, and narcissism. Plus, there is that other leg of love—the love of

God. For some this is a real turnoff as people have had bad experiences with organized religion and the churches and religious leaders who are supposedly in the God-business. In my book on gratitude, I wrote about Higher Power, a concept from Twelve Step programs.

For some, Higher Power is an easier term to deal with than "God." I quoted from Ernie Kurtz's book, *Not God: A History of Alcoholics Anonymous.* Ernie wrote that anyone or anything can be one's Higher Power, as long as it isn't oneself. For some, this idea of a Higher Power provides a way to keep the three legs of the table in view as they seek to develop good habits of self-care.

I will present different aspects that I have found helpful in committing to self-care and self-practice—a schema for understanding human experience, exercise, diet, sleep, and humor. A Reflection Question is at the end of each of these subsections.

The Seven Levels

My wife and I benefitted from the research of Ann Betz and Ursula Pottinga and the workshops we have taken with them. Ann and Ursula also work with the neuroplasticity of the brain and brain development. They created an organization called BEabove Leadership. I will describe a model they created that explains the different levels of personal, group, and organizational effectiveness. They talk about the "Seven Levels of Effectiveness" and what they call "below the line" and "above the line" attitudes.

There is a lessening of energy below the line and an increase of energy above the line. Their schema:

7. *SYNCHRONICITY* arises from an understanding that what is within us creates what is outside of us and a focus on positive experiences for all. It includes the awareness of the gift and possibility in every experience. It is the realm of "magical coincidence." Clearly, this is a favorite of mine!

6. *INNOVATION* is the ability to perceive and explore possibilities from all perspectives as well as seeking the most effective solution to issues and questions.

5. *ENGAGEMENT* is the desire to bring value to situations as well as to make a contribution, focusing on assets rather than limitations.

4. *COURAGE* is the willingness to take a stand and act against previously held beliefs and actions that tended to be disempowering.

3. FRUSTRATION is the focus on fighting and jockeying for position against others; it is more I vs. them.

2. FEAR is the belief that there is a need to protect oneself from almost certain loss, attack, and/or disappointment.

1. HOPELESSNESS is a fundamental inability to see or work for a positive future and/or outcome.

In the Seven Levels, levels 1–3 are "below the line" attitudes, while levels 5–7 are "above the line" attitudes. Level 4 is at the line; acting courageously provides the energy and movement above the line. There is more energy in acting courageously, engaging with others, innovating and creating positive energies for all.

The opposite is true in experiencing frustration, fear, and hopelessness. Self-care is seeking to stay above the line in our lives and in our dealing with others. Staying above the line increases the opportunities for developing resilience. This schema is a model for helping groups and organizations develop more and evolve into resilient cultures—that is, finding and developing ways for groups to stay above the line as well as discover ways to come back above the line when things go south "below the line."

This schema is not only a model for individuals, but is for groups also as we try to become more resilient in the face of the obstacles that come our way.

Reflection Questions

What can throw you "below the line"?

What can help you move "above the line"?

What helps you to be more courageous?

Exercise

Exercise is both physical and spiritual. I discuss spiritual exercise more in the next chapter, relating to those interior activities that focus on what gives meaning to our life— meditation, prayer, journaling, art, etc. Here we are dealing more with the ways we can exercise our bodies.

Walking, stretching, jogging are ways to stay active as well as enabling us to get up off the couch. Multiple studies show the negative effects of too much time in a sedentary position—watching television, looking at our computer screens, sitting at our desks at work, to name a few. Exercise is moving and using our bodies. My wife and I have committed to a weekly regime of Pilates, with a series of exercises to increase our core muscles. Kim Taraschi and Jennifer Thompson have been wonderful teachers for us in this area. Having a teacher can be a big help!

One of my beliefs when I began Pilates some seven years ago was expressed in the adage "no pain, no gain.". Kim disputed that, and she has helped me to see what we can gain without having to experience pain. Exercise for me has become doing Pilates and making an ongoing commitment to walk a number of times a week.

Kim taught me a helpful lesson related to the simple positioning of my wallet. For years upon years, I carried my wallet in my back pocket, and she pointed out how this threw off my posture. I now carry my wallet in my side pocket, and my posture has improved. Such shifts affect the brain as well as the body. Good physical health and physical exercise are important components of developing resilience.

Reflection Questions

What does physical exercise conjure up in your imagination? Pleasant? Painful?

How might you improve your physical exercise? Who might help you and support you?

Diet

The adage "we become what we eat" is significant. What we eat and drink impacts every level of our being. With so many different views about what constitutes a healthy diet, I am not interested in presenting one as the best for everyone. I placed diet here to say it is important to look at what we are taking into our systems by way of food and drink. When we are bogged down by unhealthy food groups and junk foods, it is more difficult to be resilient.

Clearly, obesity is a major concern in our society that impacts people's abilities to function with any energy. I compare this image with what would happen to our cars if we use lousy gas. The same is true with food and drink.

I know people who have benefitted from a Twelve Step program called Overeaters Anonymous that helps participants monitor their food usage to arrive at a more balanced diet. Others have benefitted from seeing a nutritionist or talking with their doctors.

Looking at what we eat and drink and committing to eating healthily are two ways to demonstrate self-care. These are also a way, along with exercise, to develop the stamina that is needed for resilience.

Reflection Questions

What is for you a healthy diet?

What changes might you make to follow that healthy diet?

Sleep

Another element of self-care is experiencing restful and deep sleep. Experts speak about seven to eight hours of deep sleep each evening. We are well aware of some of the obstacles to such sleep: work schedules and changing shifts, noise, uncomfortable beds, our kids not sleeping well, and many more causes. I became aware of the impact on people who either work nights or work changing schedules. It is a real challenge for them to find a regimen that allows them to sleep restfully and begin the next day with any level of energy.

This has been a challenging area for me. About six years ago, my wife noticed that I would stop breathing during the night, which concerned her. I was unaware of this. I mentioned this to my doctor, who immediately recommended that I undergo a sleep study. The results showed that I was waking up about forty times an hour. And I was immediately prescribed a sleep machine, a

CPAP machine (continuous positive airway pressure). This has made a huge difference in my sleep life. Even though I struggle with some aspects of the mask, I find I am sleeping more restfully. This has had a positive impact upon my life.

Look closely at your sleeping patterns, especially if you sleep alone. Having enough restful sleep is an important aspect of good self-care and resilience.

Reflection Questions

What's your sleep-life like?

Do you wake up tired? Refreshed?

Humor

Humor and laughter are important components of self-care and resilience. This feels especially true when we are bombarded by so much information and so many words from the social media as well as talk radio and television.

This onslaught can lead to feelings of hopelessness, fear, and frustration, taking us "below the line" in the BEabove Leadership schema. "Below the line" means a lack of energy. Laughter is one way to stay afloat and balanced. One challenge I face is learning to laugh at myself when I make a mistake instead of becoming defensive.

Practicing humor is one way to remember to laugh and laugh at myself. Watching comedies and listening to comedians are two ways to practice humor. I am a punster, and people often roll their eyes when I throw out a pun.

Punning is one way I laugh, and I hope that others will laugh with me. Some have told me that punning is one of the lowest forms of humor. That may be true; however, it's a good form of humor for me. It's a way that I can inject laughter into situations.

An important point about humor is that the focus of humor should never be aimed at laughing at or making fun of others. This type of humor is a type of bullying, whatever the age of the bully.

I remember high school days when the most "inept" or "different" people were often laughed at and made fun of. I am embarrassed in retrospect that I rarely said or did anything to defend those being laughed at or ridiculed.

The challenge with humor is to develop a sense of humor without laughing at, bullying, or scapegoating others, as well as learning to laugh at oneself.

Reflection Questions

Do you enjoy humor?

Can you laugh at yourself?

Asking for Help and Support from Others

Self-care and self-practice can often be hard for some men to do, though this can also be challenging for women in many situations. Asking for and receiving help and support from others are importance practices for developing resilience.

This is a major challenge for individuals and also for developing a culture of resilience. It is difficult to ask for help when the culture presents and affirms the image of the "rugged individualist." To develop resilience as individuals, we need to build a resilience culture in which it is okay to ask for and receive help from others. This connects to the idea of the Higher Power in the Twelve Steps—anyone or anything can be a Higher Power (other than ourselves).

An individual who supports me can be a Higher Power for me as well as a community in which I can be supported. Even support as an ideal to live up to can be a Higher Power for some people.

Asking for help and support is the bedrock for those joining support groups. Such groups often arise around a specific issue—people experience grief from the loss of a loved one, going through a divorce, dealing with cancer, struggling with unemployment, to name a few. Comfort and support are generated as people share their stories with each other. People in the group have been there before, and they share their experiences to help others.

As mentioned earlier, Twelve Step groups help their members with different kinds of addiction: alcohol, narcotics, sexuality, gambling, etc. Within these groups, it is explicitly stated there are no experts; we are sisters and brothers on a common journey. In the Twelve Step group I have belonged to for almost twenty-five years, the men in the group have been very supportive and have helped me feel somewhat normal again as they have shared their experiences and wisdom with me.

A number of professionals offer support to people struggling with different issues in their lives. Counselors and therapists help their clients become aware of where they presently are in their lives and help them make choices about what they want to do. This process works. At different times in my life, I have worked with therapists who helped me clarify what was happening in my life as well as clarifying what I wanted to do. This has been empowering.

As I struggled with the decision to leave the priesthood, a therapist helped me focus on what I truly wanted to do. Such situations of choice can often be clarified through talking with a "neutral" person who can bring some objectivity to the situation. Similar support can come from working with a life coach, a profession of which I am a member. Coaching helps individuals clarify their values and thus create actions in keeping with their values. A subgroup of coaches within life coaching, recovery life coaches, work with people in recovery from addiction. Another group includes spiritual directors who help individuals sort out their spiritual and faith issues. Other higher powers are those professionals who deal with healthy issues and concerns. This group includes medical doctors, dentists, and other types of clinicians. I have benefitted from the expertise of several in these professions. I have come to believe in the prevention model of medical care, which requires the ongoing contact with clinicians who can spot anything that seems out of the normal, identify the issues, and act upon them.

Another group of support is FRIENDS. There is incredible power and energy in friendship. This power and energy arises through the experiences of trust with friends as well as the willingness to reveal those dark places within each of us to those friends and find acceptance.

By joining support groups, seeing professionals, consulting medical professionals, and enjoying friendship, we are able to confront the debilitating effects of shame. Bréne Brown, the other wisdom figure for this chapter, has written extensively on shame and its powerful negative impact upon us. In her book, *Daring Greatly*, she describes shame, myths around shame, and how we can begin to move out of feeling shame. One experience she describes is crucial in how she has come to view shame. For many years she saw shame distinctly as a women's issue. Then one evening after a talk, a fellow came up to her and challenged her to expand her version of shame to be more inclusive. He shared that he also felt shame deeply.

The experience of shame as described by this gentleman resonates with me, especially when I am aware of when I make a mistake. For me, it is often tied with a desire (and unfair expectation) to be perfect and do things perfectly. Even though I know, in my saner moments, that perfection is impossible, the desire is strong within me to do everything perfectly. When I behave or perform in imperfect ways and make mistakes, I often feel shame, the shame that Brown so masterfully speaks about. This is a shared experience for all of us who are human. Brown is a true source of wisdom for every person, male and female, who seeks to move out of the shadows of shame and walk in the sunlight. And my experience says this is most everyone, and we are dealing with an epidemic of shame.

From my experience, feelings of guilt are a response when I feel I have done something wrong. One way to distinguish guilt and shame: I feel guilt when I feel I have made a mistake; I feel shame when I feel *I am the mistake*. Feeling shame is wanting to hide. Women and men have many different stories about how we experience shame; it is a deeply human experience that we share. We can help each other by listening to one another and not trying to fix each other. Listening is a wonderful healing experience in helping others work through shame.

When Adam and Eve were naked in the Garden of Eden, they ate of the fruit of the tree of the knowledge of good and evil and two things happened: first, they realized they were naked and clothed themselves; second, Adam blamed Eve for giving him the fruit to eat. Their "covering themselves" is a perfect image for feelings of shame—we do something we are ashamed of and we want to hide or disappear. Also often connected to shame is blame.

Blaming someone else for what we have done is way of escaping the guilt and shame of making a mistake or being "wrong." Here it was Adam blaming Eve, trying to pass the buck to someone else.

Brown speaks of a root experience of shame as "I am not enough." Aren't there many ways in our culture where we feel and experience not being enough? Not pretty or handsome enough, not successful enough, not big enough, not earning enough—simply feeling not enough! In this way, shame eats away at our attempts to be resilient and bounce back.

Brown's prescription for healing shame is to simply become vulnerable. She defines this as "uncertainty, risk and emotional exposure." (*Daring Greatly*, p. 34). Being vulnerable is not being weak; rather it is being who we are with our strengths and limitations, with our successes and failures. At its roots, becoming vulnerable is about empowering ourselves and acknowledging who we are. In Twelve Step language, this is moving us out of the powerlessness and unmanageability of Step 1.

Brown is very clear about not becoming vulnerable to everyone; rather, we share our wounds and struggles and uncertainties with a few trusted confidantes and friends. Some of the groups and professionals mentioned in this chapter are those with whom we might more easily feel vulnerable and express this vulnerability, and thus find healing.

I have found that whatever seemed like something I couldn't share with anyone, once shared with a confidant, was far easier to share with others. However, it is not necessary to share our failings and unworthiness (the feelings we are not enough) with everyone. But by sharing with a few or even only one person makes it so we are not out on the limb alone.

The way through shame is the point: to live without shame imprisoning us, we need the support and help of others, we need companions on our journeys. The word "companion" has interesting roots: *com* means "with" and *panion* comes from the Latin word *panis*, which means "bread." A companion is someone who feeds and nourishes us. We need companions on our journeys and, at times, it requires taking the risk to ask for support.

Reflection Questions

How easy it is for you to ask for support? What stands in the way?

Do you resonate with the feeling of shame?

What do you do with your shame?

CHAPTER 5

ACCENTUATE THE POSITIVE
Wisdom Figure: Jesus

A phrase Jesus often used, "Some of you say . . . but I say to you. . . ," suggests that Jesus reflected deeply upon life experience. In speaking of Jesus, Paul says: "He did not cling to his equality with God, but emptied himself to assume the condition of a slave and became as men are." (Philippians 2:6–7) In John's Gospel, Jesus said to Mary Magdalene: "Do not cling to me." (John 20:17). Though the circumstances in each of these passages differ, I interpret his advice to "not cling" as an entreaty to instead reach out, claim positivity, and embrace our own resilience; being willing to let go of our own self-doubt, negative judgments, regrets, and resentments.

Jesus didn't preach a lot of "Do nots." Again and again, he proclaimed the positive: love of God, neighbor, and self, and the importance of forgiving others. Peter asked Jesus, "How often must I forgive my brother if he wrongs me? As often as seven times?" and Jesus responded,

"Not seven but seventy-seven times." (Matthew 18:21–22) In these words of Jesus, I would much prefer "humans" for "men" and "brothers and sisters" rather than "brothers."

My wife and I were at a play, *The Sisters of Peace*, which detailed the lives of four extraordinary women: the McDonald sisters from St Paul, Minnesota. They are sisters by blood and sisters within a religious community, the Sisters of St Joseph. Passionately committed to working for peace their entire lives, they embody Jesus's call for us to courageously live positive values.

In the discussion after the play, the four sisters sang the song, "Ac-Cent-Tchu-Ate the Positive," a popular 1944 song by Harold Arlen and Johnny Mercer, that contains ideal advice for building resilience by latching onto the positive in life and spreading joy, eliminating the negative and minimizing gloom, and not even bothering with "Mister in-Between"—just like Jonah in the whale and Noah in the ark did when everything looked so dark! I suspect this song mirrors how these women lived their lives. Jonah and Noah each faced huge odds and came through successfully.

Hearing these "sisters" sing this song just as I was beginning to write this chapter struck me as another moment of synchronicity. And it connected with another event that took place in January of this year that helped me focus further. I mentioned earlier that I met Gregg Braden as the result of a question I asked body worker Mike Fricke, knowing that he was a curious kind of a guy, and he didn't disappoint me. He said he and his wife were into a way of meditation created by Braden, and the rest is history. This ended up leading me to discover another book he wrote about, of all things, *Resilience from the Heart: The Power to Thrive in Life's Extremes.*

Gregg Braden is a prolific writer and thinker who makes the connection again and again between resilience and accentuating the positive. In *Resilience from the Heart,* he talks about a pioneering organization called HeartMath Institute that conducts research on "the human heart psychophysiology of stress, emotions, and the interactions between the heart and brain. [2] HeartMath research shows that the patterns of heart activity related to different emotions have "distinct effects on cognitive and emotional function," and that the ability to sustain positive emotions benefits our entire body in significant ways. We can learn how to generate "increased heart rhythm coherence."

For Braden, to create this heart/brain coherence will open us to becoming aware of the truth that uniquely

[2] See more at https://www.heartmath.com/science/.

resides in each of our hearts. In this coherence, he sees two sources for knowledge and truth: the brain in our heads and the "little" brain that resides in our hearts. He describes the heart and the brain as the body's master organs that work together, "two separate organs connected through a common network of information."

I invite you to keep in mind his goal of promoting this coherence or integration between the brain and the heart as we explore how to accentuate the positive.

Centering Prayer and Mindfulness

Gregg Braden developed a meditation method that is fairly similar to other meditation methods. He includes a centering prayer as well as mindfulness practices.

I have been practicing his simple meditation method ever since I saw him demonstrate it on a YouTube video. Several versions of his meditations are available online. The simple method consists of two steps.

Step 1: Heart Focus

This step involves shifting the focus of our attention to the region of the heart and breathing a little more slowly than usual. I have found it to be helpful to place a hand over my heart region to draw my focus and attention to my heart.

Step 2: Activate a Positive Feeling

This step involves calling up a positive feeling such as appreciation or compassion or gratitude. Feeling and sustaining these positive feelings help to maintain an optimal quality of conversation between our heart and our brain.

I invite you to try this method of meditating along with any other ways of meditating that you have found helpful. Some kind of meditation or centering experience can be very helpful in shifting our attitudes from negativity to positivity, and there are many ways besides this technique to meditate, become centered, or become mindful.

A method for centering prayer was pioneered by Fr Thomas Keating, who emphasized the importance of listening in praying, leaving space to listen to God and not just tell God what to do. Listening while in prayer balances all the words we have prayed over the years in various traditions.

Jesus said, "And in your prayers, do not babble as the pagans do, for they think by using many words they will be make themselves heard . . . your Father knows what you need before you ask." (Matthew 6:7) My experience is that it is not only the pagans who use lots of words to pray;

it is also folks who call themselves Christians!

These ways of meditating and centering are similar to practices that help bring about mindfulness. Developing mindfulness is becoming aware of what is happening in the here and now. I have found in my own experience that it is so easy to get lost in the past, full of regrets and resentments for what happened or what didn't take place. We can just as easily get lost in the future, feeling anxiety about what "might" happen tomorrow or how to deal with something that might or might not come about. This corresponds with a truth from the Twelve Steps: take life one day at a time and live in the present moment.

In all of these methods, the emphasis is on practice: develop a practice or practices that enable us to listen more, to live more in the present moment, and be more in tune with the truth that comes from the brain in our heart.

A word of caution if you decide to practice Braden's heart meditation in public: on a number of occasions as I practiced this method, placing my hand over my heart and closing my eyes, people have asked me in alarm, "Are you all right?"

Seeing me this way, they thought I was in some distress or having a heart attack. The paradox here is that I was doing the opposite—trying to strengthen my heart connection. Things are not always as they seem!

Finding Communities of Support

I spoke earlier about the positive impact created by being part of something larger than oneself. It is important to belong, whatever that might look like. I found a meditation on the internet that was inspired by Paramahansa Yogananda, entitled "Dare to be Different," which referred to a single drop of water.

Separate from the mighty and strong ocean, a drop of water will be lost . . . but the same drop of water in the company of other drops of water gathers strength. Billions of drops of water gather to form the great and mighty ocean.

This image resonates with an image that my mentor, Ira Progoff, used in creating and leading workshops in journal-keeping. His sense of community emphasized the importance of allowing people privacy as they wrote in their journals. At the same time, there was an energy of support created as people journaled together.

One of Progoff's favorite lines was the importance of staying out of other people's lives. His definition of community emphasized each person's uniqueness and individuality. At the same time, we need communities to stay alive and grow. Like in so many things, it is not either/or, it is both/and.

There are multiple possibilities for belonging in supportive communities. What works for one person doesn't necessarily work for another. Some find their families as very important communities of support, while others do not. Some find their families to be sources of frustration, abandonment, and hurt—resembling war zones.

My parents died a long time ago, and my only sibling died some sixteen years ago. I have found "family" in the Dominican community I belonged to for many years and also in the family my wife and I have created, which also includes family members of the next generation.

Jesus said. "His mother and his brothers came looking for him, but they could not get to him because of the crowd. He was told, 'Your mother and your brothers are standing outside and want to see you.' But he said in answer, 'My mother and my brothers are those who hear the word of God and put it into practice.'" (Luke 8:19–21) I bet there were also sisters in the family group that came!

A couple of ideas have intrigued me for some time in regard to this passage. First, Jesus redefined family beyond just the flesh-and-blood connections. This might be one of the more significant things Jesus discussed and modeled. Second, the basis for family is listening. We create family bonds through listening and being present to one another.

This can be our family or a religious or spiritual community, a support group, a Twelve Step group, and on and on. These communities can be of the same gender (my wife and I have each belonged to communities of the same gender) or of different genders.

The bottom line is being willing to listen to one another, support one another, and affirm one another is what constitutes family. We are all yearning for communities where we can be heard and be ourselves—in Bréne Brown's words—places where we can safely become vulnerable, and where we hear words of welcome.

I am heartened whenever I think of the words that are the motto of the Catholic community my wife and I belong to in south Minneapolis called St. Joan of Arc Church. The motto is simply: "We welcome you wherever you are on your journey!"

This motto was created several years ago by the pastor, Fr Bill Murtaugh, as the Church was shifting the parish house to a house where people with AIDs could come for support. The motto was his way of stretching the community to be sensitive to and welcoming of others who are different from us. And the motto has stuck!

Supportive communities do not have to be large in numbers. Jesus said: "Where two or three are gathered in my name, I am there." (Matthew 18:20) Two people are enough to have a community. It is interesting that Jesus didn't say, "I want a thousand to be present before I show up."

No, he spoke of two or three. It is time to let go of numbers in determining the success of events or projects or communities. Let's instead focus on quality, not quantity. Belonging and contributing to communities of support helps us remain in positivity, as Braden suggests.

Self-Affirmation and the Affirmation of Others

As I reflected upon this section, I found myself thinking of the words of a man I never thought I'd ever quote, who said, "When elected, I will drain the swamp."

"Swamp" is an apt metaphor for where we all are in the world, and the swamp is filled with guilt, shame, regrets, disappointments, resentments, anxieties, as well as other negative emotions and experiences. Many of us are drowning in the swamps of our lives.

How then, do we drain the swamp?

My suggestion is to discover multiple ways to affirm

ourselves as well as affirming others. What might this look like? One way I have find helpful is to keep on hand some short expressions of positive affirmation that we can say to ourselves when we feel we are heading into the swamp.

"I am okay."

"I will be okay."

"I am a creative person."

"I am where I am meant to be."

"I can figure out a way to work this challenging situation."

"People do care about me."

How can we express affirmation to those around us? An example is apt from my first book. Someone pointed out that I attributed a quote to the wrong Roosevelt; it was Teddy, not Franklin, who spoke of daring greatly.

I felt myself begin to descend into my own personal swamp of perfectionism and shame.

Then what came to me was: "Yes, I made a mistake, and my book is not perfect."

That's a fact! So I admitted my error and told others that I didn't want my mistake to cloud the message of the book or suggest blame on anyone else's part. Taking responsibility helped to dissipate the shame I felt.

A favorite line of mine from Twelve Step literature:

It's about progress, not perfection. I see affirming oneself as a way of practicing progress by acknowledging mistakes and missed opportunities, and moving on. This is another way to develop the resilience to get up and not get stuck in failings.

In addition to self-affirmation is what I call "resistance" work. For me "resistance" work entails refraining from going along with the crowd and whatever the crowd is saying and/or doing. This has come to mean that I limit how much time I watch the news and listen to talk radio.

I found that listening to these sources only created more agitation in me as well as heightened feelings of powerlessness and anxiety. Another way to affirm myself means committing to resisting to what others are saying and doing.

An aside here: When I mentioned to one of the people to whom this book is dedicated (Tom O'Meara) that I was writing a book on resilience, he thought I said resistance. His comment led me to think about the relationship between resistance and resilience—at times, in order to be resilient, we have to resist the pressures and expectations of others.

Thank you again, Tom!

Compassion

Another way to accentuate the positive and develop resilience flows from the meditation that Gregg Braden created, which emphasizes the power of positive emotions. These emotions include feeling compassion and concern for others. I see compassion as inviting us to stretch and look beyond ourselves. The word "compassion" has two Latin roots: *com* meaning "with" and *passion* coming from a Latin verb *patior*, meaning "to suffer." This is also the root for patience. From its roots, then, compassion is really a willingness to suffer and be patient with others. The patience piece can often be a real challenge for me.

The sufferings of others can help us realize how much we have to be grateful for. Jesus told a story in the Gospel of Luke 10:25–37: A Jewish person is robbed and left in a ditch. Several Jewish people see him and walk by him, each having a good reason why they couldn't stop and help. Finally a person does stop, and he happens to be a person who is an enemy of the Jewish people, a Samaritan. He helps the Jewish person, literally, to get back on his feet and paid for whatever was needed for him to get better.

Jesus ends the story by asking a question: "Hey, who was neighbor to this fellow in the ditch?"

The answer: "the Good Samaritan."

As he frequently does, Jesus turned the tables on the people listening to him (those are trying to trick him), saying the hero of the story, then, is the enemy; while the Jewish folks who saw him, walked on by. Another example of a marvelous teacher!

I think Jesus is saying not to let gender, sexual orientation, ethnicity, religion, or any other difference stand in the way of reaching out to others and showing mercy and compassion. Being compassionate is more important than all the religious rules that humans have created over the eons and continue to do so.

What might this mean practically to you and me?

In a society that is polarized and divided along all sorts of lines, can we move beyond "just hanging out with our own?" A popular bumper sticker speaks of doing "random acts of kindness." Acts of kindness bring positivity both to ourselves and to others.

A concrete act of kindness I mentioned earlier is to learn people's names and call people by their names—whether at church or on the softball fields. I learned years ago that, even if I am wrong and call a person by the wrong name, people appreciate that I made an effort to address them by name. And if I forget a name, I remember better the second or third time when they tell me their name. I don't always have to be right to be positive! Calling people by name helps create a culture of resilience where people are known and not just passed by like the guy in the ditch that Jesus mentioned.

Another example comes to mind from an event that happened many years ago. A friend of mine told me he was gay. I listened and didn't panic or run away. I accepted Paul. The next day he shared with me that he feared that I would disconnect from him when he told me he was gay. I responded with something like, "Paul, how could I disconnect from you as you are my friend. You were there when my mother died and supported me."

Many years later the issue of gay marriage surfaced in Minnesota in terms of changing the law to allow gays to marry. I was faced with a dilemma—how could I support gay marriage and not draw the wrath of the Archbishop at that time who was totally opposed to gay marriage?

I decided I would do this by showing up at meetings that were in favor of gay marriage. What usually happened was that we were invited to share a significant story that led us to support gay marriage. Many times I talked about my friend Paul. What has struck me is that it is very hard to condemn someone or disconnect from them if we know them, just like Paul and me. If we only spend our time with others just like us, it is easy to fall into camps that tend to demonize those who are different.

Random acts of kindness and compassion invite us at times to leave our comfort zones and discover that others are often in an even more challenging and difficult place than we are. This includes at times reaching out to people on the other side from us politically. This reaching out and stretching build resilience and contribute to feelings of positivity.

Choosing rather than Reacting

Another element for developing positivity and resilience rests upon making choices, rather than just reacting to situations and people. Choices can be about very little things or the biggest of all things. The main point is that we choose, while remaining aware that we will probably not always make the right choice. Neuroscience, the focus of BEabove Leadership, speaks of the good effects that come from making choices. One such good effect is the releasing of dopamine in the brain. Dopamine is an important neurotransmitter that facilitates communication between the nerve cells in the brain and positively influences our pleasure and reward centers. Experiencing dopamine makes it easier to do what we did again and again. This is important in choosing to do certain things and not do others. Making choices slows us down and gives us a chance at times to be able to see the bigger picture, rather than just reacting to what presents itself.

In this regard is an axiom from a philosophy class I took back in the sixties: "first in intention, last in execution." What this stresses in regard to making choices is the importance of choosing an intention before taking action, and being intentional about what we are going to do.

I am a big believer in "to do" lists. They provide me with a focus and intention for what I am going to do (and what I want to do). Though "to do" lists are not for everyone, they have become important to me, especially when having completed a task, I am able to cross it off my list. I feel a sense of accomplishment!

This type of triumph also provides dopamine for the brain, which feels good. My "to do" lists enable me to more easily choose positivity and see my accomplishments, which also contributes to feeling more resilient.

Spreading Positivity

Positivity is infectious! Gregg Braden speaks about energy fields in an article, "The Magnetic Field of the Heart." He reports about how people responded to the 9/11 attacks. Satellites 22,000 miles in space registered the changes in the magnetic field of the earth as humans responded to the tragedy through the images everyone was seeing. Our positive feelings of care, compassion, appreciation, gratitude, etc., created a magnetic field inside our bodies that was part of the magnetic field of our planet! And the scientists were able to see it!

That we are affected by others and others affect us bring back images of *Mr. Rogers' Neighborhood*. We have an impact upon others in the energy fields of our lives as individuals and as part of a community. Consider how this impact can be positive or negative. If you walk into a house where people are smoking and spend time in that environment, our clothes smell of smoke even after we leave. The smoke has become "part of us." What happens to you when you spend time with people who are critical and negative? We are strongly affected by those around us. I have found that it is difficult to stay positive when I am in a negative environment/field of energy. And we can spread positivity to others by being positive, feeling positive feelings.

In his article "From Competition to Cooperation: An Emerging World Order," Braden explores the differences in energy fields when people cooperate and collaborate. Strong positive energies are released when people cooperate and work together. Archeological records document civilizations that survived transitions when they cooperated; whereas civilizations that collapsed were those that responded to transitions with fear, aggression, and intense competition. Sounds challenging for us today, doesn't it?

We have a choice that has implications for ourselves and for Earth. Will we choose ways to collaborate? Or will we compete with each other to win no matter the cost? My sense is that we are at a place where an ongoing commitment to winning is ultimately leading to everyone losing!

Positivity is infectious in a life-giving way and is foundational for developing our resilience individually and as a culture. I am more resilient in the company of positive people. This reflects what neuroscientists know about mirroring neurons: our brains are affected by the energies and postures of those around us. We are not neutral!

We make choices about what comes our way, and those choices impact our resilience as well. Choosing to accentuate the positive is very good for you, for me, and for everyone, including the earth!

Developing a Practice of Gratitude

Last but not least, developing a practice of gratitude contributes to feelings of positivity and also contributes to resiliency. It probably does not come as much of a surprise to those who remember my first book to see me bringing gratitude back into the mix. Since writing the book about gratitude, I have been struck by the many people who talk about the positives that grow out of a practice of regularly giving thanks. It's an idea and practice that has come of age! And it is very simple to do!

I came to rediscover gratitude through praying the Serenity Prayer, a staple of the Twelve Step movement. I was struck that the three main prayers were requests—asking for serenity, courage, and wisdom. I just felt this prayer should also include giving thanks for what we have received. Giving thanks closes the loop begun in the asking. That was where I began my journey of gratitude, and I discovered that others had also been looking into this topic and had done extensive research. Dr. Robert Emmons, a professor of psychology who has taught and written about gratitude, has shown the positive effects of regularly giving thanks for what we have been given. One effect is that people who regularly give thanks are happier and healthier people.

Two points in regard to giving thanks: the first is what Gregg Braden talks about in his heart meditation when he invites people to meditate on positive feelings like appreciation, gratitude, and compassion. This is an alternative to being satisfied with the status quo or a limited view of things. Positivity engenders more positivity. Appreciating what we have leads to feeling grateful for all that we have been given.

The second point is that gratitude is a two-way street. One side is giving thanks to others for what others have given us; the other side is a willingness to receive the gratitude of others. It can be deflating to hear someone say in response to expressions of gratitude, "Oh, it was nothing."

How do we receive the gratitude of others? Please ponder this important aspect of deepening a culture of both gratitude and resilience.

Another dimension of gratitude is the experience of celebration—acknowledging and celebrating what we have done by way of our accomplishments. People have sometimes shared with me that they didn't feel worthy to celebrate their accomplishments. There is certainly some shame reflected in these responses.

I urge everyone to think about finding ways to

celebrate what you have done. Celebrating what we have done opens the door to gratitude—who can we be grateful to for all the things we have accomplished?

The last point I want to add about gratitude relates to prayer. Giving thanks and receiving the thanks of others are ways to pray. Gregg Braden raises this in his book, *Secret of the Lost Mode of Prayer: The Hidden Power of Beauty, Blessing, Wisdom, and Hurt.* What I hear him saying is that simple experiences like appreciating beauty, giving a blessing, discovering wisdom, and acknowledging hurts are all ways to pray.

These types of prayer can happen in day-to-day life and do not require going to a synagogue, mosque, or church. They happen in ordinary life if we have the eyes to see and the ears to hear.

Braden is also a firm believer in all of us being connected as we live in a field of energy where we are able to impact others and others are able to impact us. From this perspective, prayer is sending positive energies into the universe. He believes this is a lost form of prayer.

We have touched many bases in emphasizing the importance of positivity in building resilient spirits—meditation, centering prayer and practices of mindfulness, finding communities of support, self-affirmation as well as affirming others, developing compassion and kindness, choosing to choose and not just simply reacting to situations and people, and developing a practice of gratitude. These are all powerful building blocks of resilience.

Reflection Questions

Which of the building blocks of positivity do you practice now? Which would you like to develop?

How positive are you? What disrupts your positivity?

How do you affirm yourself?

Where do you find a community or communities of support?

How will you choose to accentuate resilience in your life?

EPILOGUE

This book was truly a work in progress and, really, isn't that what life is—a work in progress? Hopefully, we learn as we move along and continue to have new life experiences. Many moons ago I began this venture with an idea of writing a book on resilience, and then events happened: snowstorms, falling on the ice, a car accident, my mother-in-law dying at the age of ninety-nine, and many other events. All of these events impacted what I wrote as well as challenged my resilience—my ability to get up and keep going. This is what life does to and for us.

Resilience is truly a response to the events of life: the kinds of experiences that affirm us, as well as those that challenge us to our core. In conclusion, I want to underline the importance of mastery and support in developing resilience. Resilience is in part a result of genetics. And in a larger way, it is the result of many choices we make. Having a sense that we have some control over our lives and our situations as well as having support from others are two areas we can further develop and work on. I sense it is important that we teach these areas to others, especially young people who are still learning what life is all about. We develop our resilience by teaching these skills to others.

Resilience can often be the wild card that emerges from doing such things as continuing to learn, being part of supportive communities, accentuating the positive, eating healthy foods, and exercising. Resilience is often the 3 that comes from adding 1 plus 1. It is the "something more" that is vitally important to our future as individuals and as communities. We often can't control what comes our way; we can control how we choose to respond to what comes our way. That is resilience!

Consider the words of the visionary writer Malcolm Gladwell in his book *The Tipping Point: How Little Things Can Make a Big Difference.* We never know when we are at a tipping point—the moment when things shift in a big way. Aren't all of us at a tipping point in regard to resilience? I think so!

Will we proceed with our beliefs and hopes that, in community with others, we can create a more resilient world and culture where we can support others and others can support us in living with more resilience?

For me this is working to create a more compassionate world, stretching to reach out to others.

This is the kind of world in which resilience can be found.

I urge you to keep believing, hoping, and loving—such is the stuff of resilience!

I conclude with my favorite prayer—with a slight addition . . .

God, grant me the *Serenity* to accept the things I cannot change,

the *Courage* to change the things that I can,

and the *Wisdom* to know the difference.

I am *Grateful* for the serenity, courage, and wisdom you have given me, along with the *Resilience* you have accorded me.

ANNOTATED BIBLIOGRAPHY
&
SUGGESTED READING LIST

Betz, CPCC, Ann, and Ursula Pottinga, CPCC. *BEabove Leadership: The Art and Science of Human Transformation* See https://www.beaboveleadership.com.
[Betz and Pottinga give information about the seven levels and neuroplasticity and their impact upon us.]

Braden, Gregg. "From Competition to Cooperation: An Emerging World Order." August 31, 2012. See https://www.youtube.com/watch?v=BjtREE1zHx8. [Braden contrasts the positive energy released when humans cooperate and the opposite effect when humans react from fearful places and compete.]

Braden, Gregg. *Resilience from the Heart: The Power to Thrive in Life's Extremes.* Carlsbad: Hay House Publishing, 2015. [Braden focuses on the importance of opening to the knowledge that comes from the brain and the heart and how important this is in developing resilience.]

Braden, Gregg. *Secrets of the Lost Mode of Prayer: The Hidden Power of Beauty, Blessing, Wisdom, and Hurt.* Carlsbad: Hay House Publishing, 2006.
[Braden chronicles his search for ancient forms of prayer, and the importance of creating our own prayers, which can ground our developing resilience.]

Braden, Gregg. "The Magnetic Field of the Heart." *School of the Deep Heart.*
See https://schoolofthedeepheart.com/teachings/the-science-of-the-heart/4-the-magnetic-field-of-the-heart-by-gregg-braden and http://www.gregbraden.com.
[Braden develops his research and reflection upon our living in energy fields, not just as isolated individuals.]

Brown, Bréne. *Daring Greatly: How the Courage to be Vulnerable Transforms the Way We Live, Love. Parent and Lead.* USA: Penguin Putnam, Inc., 2012.
[Brown explores experiences of the author and others, and the importance of vulnerability in moving through shame, an obstacle to developing resilience.]

Brown, Bréne. *Braving the Wilderness: The Quest for True Belonging and the Courage to Stand Alone.* New York: Random House, 2017.
[Brown describes the importance of living in the paradox of being alone and belonging and important aspects of developing resilience.]

Brown, Bréne. *Dare to Lead: Brave Work, Tough Conversations. Whole Hearts.* New York City: Random House Publishing Group, 2017.
[Developing resilience and acting resiliently can often be brave and tough work and involve tough conversations as we seek to resist just going along with the crowd.]

Clark, Glenn. *The Man Who Talks with the Flowers: The Life Story of Dr. George Washington Carver.* Austin MN: Macalester Park Publishing Company, 2010.
[This exquisite small book about the life of George Washington Carver describes how he survived major odds to make great contributions to humankind.]

Cummins, PhD, Denise. "Why Some People Are More Resilient than Others." *Psychology Today,* March 2015. See https://www.psychologytoday.com/us/blog/good-thinking/201503/why-some-people-are-more-resilient-others.

[A Heather Rusch study illustrates that a sense of mastery and support are key ingredients for developing resilience.]

Duhig, Charles. *The Power of Habit: Why We Do What We Do in Life and Business.* New York: Random House, 2012.

[The author describes the power of habits in our lives and how difficult it is to change habits, especially longstanding ones, and he sheds light on the challenges as we try to change habits in order to become more resilient.]

Emmons, Robert. *Gratitude Works!: A 21-Day Program for Creating Emotional Prosperity.* San Francisco: Jossey-Bass, 2013.

[This book is the work of a pioneer researcher on the positive effects of developing a regular practice of gratitude.]

Graham, Linda. *Resilience: Powerful Practices for Bouncing Back from Disappointment, Difficulty and even Disaster.* Novato CA: New World Library, 2018.
[Suggests practices for those interested in developing resilience.]

Gladwell, Malcolm. *The Tipping Point: How Little Things Can Make a Big Difference.* Boston: Little, Brown and Company, 2000.
[Presents interesting perspectives on life and talks about how many small steps can lead to a major tipping point, a major change in perspective or ways of living. This image is helpful in terms of the small steps that can lead to becoming more resilient.]

Hanson, Rick. *Resilient: Find Your Inner Strength.* London: Rider, 2018.
[Points to the importance of resilience in developing a person's inner strength.]

HeartMath Institute. Heartmath.com. HeartMath, 14700 West Park Ave, Boulder Creek, CA 95006. See https://www.heartmath.com/.

[HeartMath research and publications point to ways of achieving heart coherence; an important experience is living with more positivity and therefore with greater resilience.]

Kurtz, Ernie. *Not God: A History of Alcoholics Anonymous.* Center City, MN: Hazelden Publishing, 1991.
[Ideas about who/what can be a person's Higher Power; demystifies Higher Power to some degree.)

Obama, Michelle. *Becoming.* New York: Crown Publishing Group, 2018.
[Excellent book on ways to develop resilience in the face of major challenges.]

Progoff, Ira. *At a Journal Workshop: The Basic Text and Guide for Using the Intensive Journal.* New York: Dialogue House Library, 1975.
[A whole new way of keeping a journal by my mentor to whom I owe a great deal.]

Progoff, Ira. *Jung, Synchronicity and Human Destiny.* New York: Dell Delta, 1973.
[About the author's time with Carl Jung, a springboard to develop his own ideas around synchronicity.]

Rinder, Mike. "Neuroplasticity." *Something Can Be Done About It* blog article, April 22, 2019. https://www.mikerindersblog.org/neuroplasticity/ [Interesting ideas about how the brain works and what can help develop resilience.]

Scannell, Mark. *The Gratitude Element: A New Look at the Serenity Prayer.* Minneapolis: Gasscann Publishers, 2015. [Gratitude emerges as an important addition to the Serenity Prayer.]

Southwick, Steven, and Dennis Chaney. "The Science of Resilience: Implications for the Prevention and Treatment of Depression." *Science Magazine,* October, 2015. [Research speaks about differences in people in relation to resilience and how people are more resilient than they think. Expectations are extremely important in what happens to us.]

ACKNOWLEDGMENTS

As noted at the beginning of this book, I especially acknowledge four people who each in their own way taught me about resilience and helped me become more resilient. I am grateful to Bob, Stu, Tom, and Elaine. I am also grateful to the people I mentioned in this book who have taught me much about life and resilience.

I am grateful to Marly Cornell, my editor for the second time, whose insights and suggestions were most helpful in arriving at this final manuscript. Thanks also to Marie Thielen, a longtime friend, colleague, and artist for her photograph that graces the cover of this book. Thanks also to Elder Carson, who designed the cover for this book.

Giving thanks is forever a good thing and so thank you to all who have contributed to this book in one way or another.

ABOUT THE AUTHOR

Originally from Oak Park, Illinois, a suburb of Chicago, Mark Scannell attended the University of Notre Dame for two years before joining a religious community of priests and brothers, called the Dominican Order. He was ordained a Roman Catholic priest in 1969 and became the recruiter for this community. During this time, he met a person who became a mentor to him, Dr. Ira Progoff, who had created a journaling process called the Intensive Journal, which Mark taught for many years. He left the priesthood in 1984 and married Elaine Gaston in 1985.

Mark has worked as a consultant, counselor, and a co-owner of a manufacturer's representative plumbing company. He is a certified life coach with a specialty in coaching people working with their addictions. Since retiring from the plumbing business, Mark enjoys officiating at weddings, umpiring softball, and deepening friendships. He also enjoys the supportive and challenging community of St Joan of Arc in south Minneapolis, Minnesota.

Mark enjoys the awareness of synchronistic experiences in his life and in the lives of others that point to the presence of a Higher Power. He is grateful for the opportunity to write his previous book, *The Gratitude Element: A New Look at the Serenity Prayer* (available on Amazon.com) and to write this book on resilience, which have provided him with opportunities to talk with people about the ideas in these books and continue his ongoing learning process.

Mark and his wife Elaine live in Minneapolis, Minnesota, and enjoy the youth and vitality of their nieces and nephews as well as their great nieces and great nephews. He considers it wonderful and life-giving to give thanks!

∞

In the interest of ongoing learning, Mark invites you to share your insights and questions with him.

gasscann@bitstream.net

www.thegratitudeelement.com

612.387.3778

Thank you in advance for chances to dialogue!

∞

The Gratitude Element: A New Look at the Serenity Prayer by Mark Scannell (2015) Gasscann Publishers, Minneapolis

The author poses an addition to the Serenity Prayer inspired by his experiences praying this prayer over many years. Doesn't it make sense to give thanks after asking and receiving what we asked for and received? Expressing gratitude regularly leads to a happier way of living.

What readers say about *The Gratitude Element . . .*

"This book is an engaging, thoughtful reflection on a classic prayer. The book includes 12-Step and biblical references along with real-life examples from the author's own journey. Nicely done. I am grateful for *The Gratitude Element.*" —Angelo Gentile

"A no nonsense, must read, which helps me refocus my priorities." —Michael Halley

"A lucid and elegant presentation that gives a new dimension to the Serenity Prayer." —Michael Pearman

"A thought-provoking guide – essential and useful for any Twelve Step group, spirituality group or wisdom study group." —Jon Schwabach

"This book demonstrates Mark's gift for presenting something simply without simplifying it." —Dick Rice

The Gratitude Element is available on Amazon.com

Further information about Mark Scannell

In addition to being the author of *The Gratitude Element: A New Look at the Serenity Prayer* and *Resilience: The Ability to Rebound from Adversity*, Mark is available as a speaker on the topics of gratitude and resilience. He has spoken to groups of various sizes seeking to increase their knowledge around these themes.

Mark offers his services in helping couples plan their wedding ceremonies, and he officiates at wedding ceremonies.

As a life coach, Mark helps individuals discover what is of true value to them and helps people identify the actions that can help them embody those values.

For any of the above services, Mark can be reached by phone @ 612-387-3778 or through e-mail at gasscann@bitstream.net.

Made in the USA
Columbia, SC
18 August 2019